Why is Night Dark?

Sophy Tahta

Designed by Christopher Gillingwater, Kim Blundell and Lindy Dark
Illustrated by Guy Smith, Joseph McEwan and Brin Edwards
Science consultant: Sue Becklake
Cover design by Russell Punter
Cover illustration by Christyan Fox
With thanks to Sarah Cronin

CONTENTS

Dark nights

In this book you can find out why night is dark. But there is a lot more to know about night and what happens then. Here are some things you may have noticed. They are all explained later on.

Have you ever noticed that the Moon can be different shapes?

On a clear night you can see lots of stars. Do you know what happens to them during the day?

Sometimes the Moon and stars are hidden by clouds or fog. They are still there, even though you cannot see them.

Town lights

Electric lights in towns or cities can also make it seem less dark at night.

If you live in a town or city, you may have noticed how the sky glows at night.

All the lights you see here run on electricity. Have you ever wondered how electric light bulbs work?

 Pictures with the symbol can be downloaded from ***www.usborne-quicklinks.com***

Did you know?

When it is day where you are, it is night on the other side of the world.

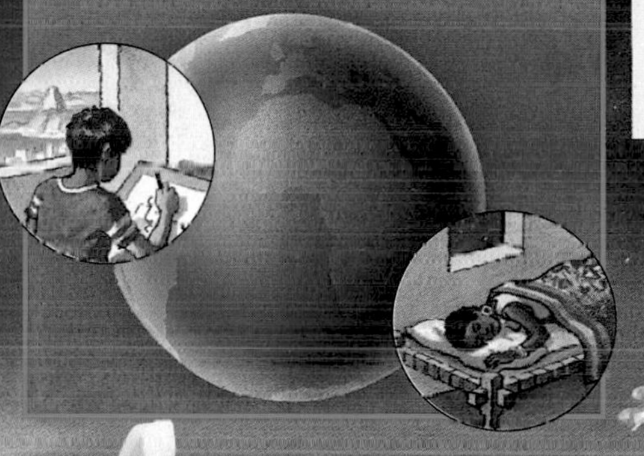

As you go to bed some animals are waking up. They sleep in the day and look for food at night.

Do you know how these animals find their way in the dark?

The Sun never sets here in summer. It is called the midnight Sun.

Some places do not get dark at night in summer, or get light during the day in winter.

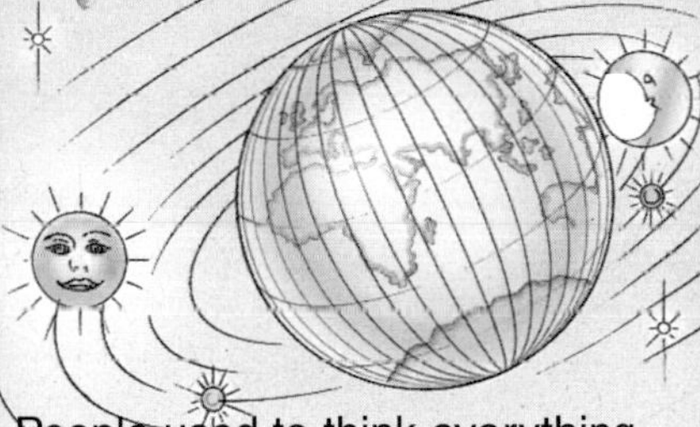

People used to think everything in space moved around the Earth. They invented reasons to explain night and dark. In this book you can find out what really happens.

Light and dark

It would always be dark on Earth if the Sun did not rise every morning. The Sun gives us light each day.

The Sun is a giant ball of incredibly hot, glowing gases. It gives out a huge amount of light and heat. Without it nothing could live or grow on Earth.

The Sun always shines, even when clouds stop you from seeing it.

A chariot of fire

The Sun is so important to life on Earth that hundreds of years ago people worshipped it as a god.

The Ancient Greeks believed that their Sun god Helios drove his chariot across the sky in the day. He rested his horses at night.

The Sun in the sky

On sunny days you can see the Sun rise, move across the sky and set.*

People used to think this was because the Sun moved around the Earth.

In the morning the Sun rises in one part of the sky.

At midday you can see the Sun high above you.

In the evening the Sun sets in another part of the sky.

*NEVER STARE AT THE SUN. IT CAN DAMAGE YOUR EYES.

The spinning Earth

Now people know that the Sun does not move around the Earth. It is really the Earth that spins around and around in space.

The Sun only shines on one half of the spinning Earth.

The half facing the Sun is in the light. It is daytime there.

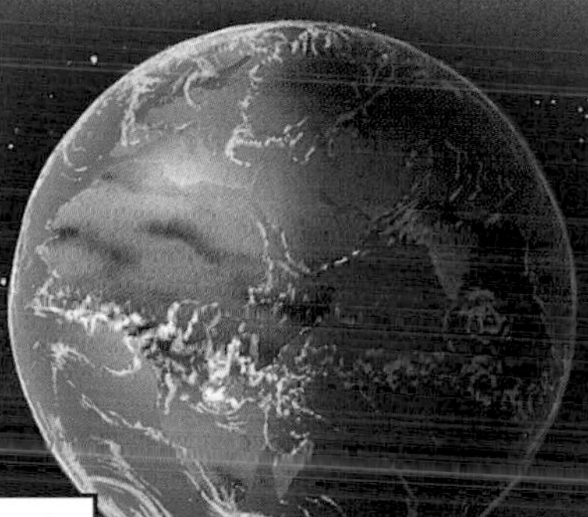

The sunlight cannot reach the other half of the Earth.

The half facing away from the Sun is in the dark. It is night there.

Sunrise and sunset

As your part of the Earth turns towards the Sun it begins to get light. This is when the Sun seems to rise.

As your part of the Earth turns away from the Sun, it begins to get dark. This is when the Sun seems to set.

See for yourself

You need a torch and a ball. Mark a spot on the ball for your home with tape or a pen. Make your room dark.

Ask someone to turn the ball while you shine the torch on it. See how the spot goes in and out of the light.

Hold the ball at the top and bottom and turn it this way.

Internet link *Go to* ***www.usborne-quicklinks.com*** *for a link to a website where you can see what happens when the sun sets and it gets dark.*

Day turns to night

The Earth makes one full spin every 24 hours. During this time most places have a day and a night.

But not all places have day and night at the same time. As one place spins into the light, another spins out of it.

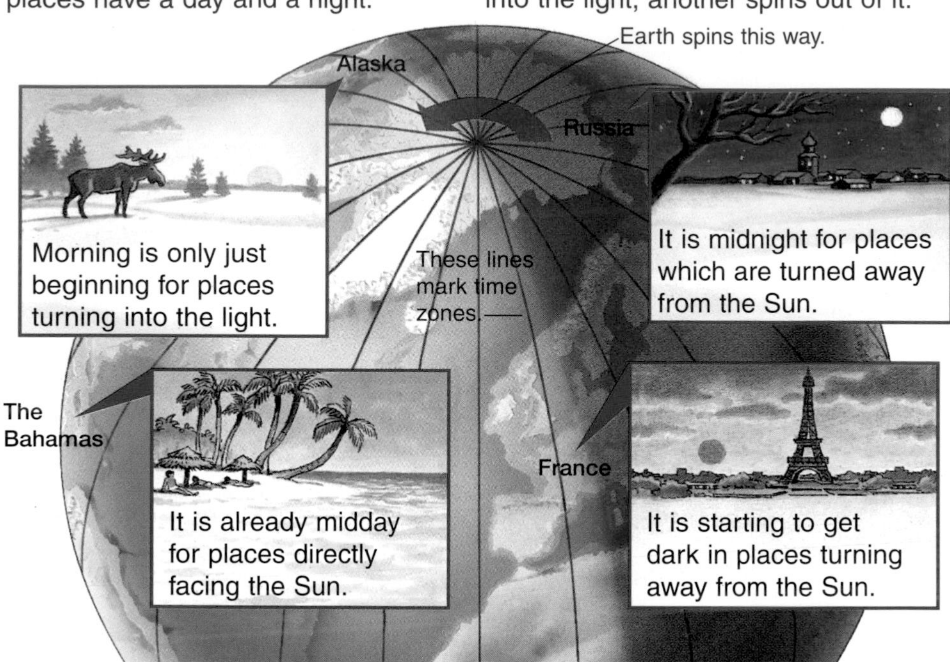

Earth spins this way.
Alaska
Russia
Morning is only just beginning for places turning into the light.
These lines mark time zones.
It is midnight for places which are turned away from the Sun.
The Bahamas
France
It is already midday for places directly facing the Sun.
It is starting to get dark in places turning away from the Sun.

Sometimes we need to know what time it is in another country. To help us, people have divided the world into 24 "slices" called time zones.

You can see them in this picture. Each place in one zone has the same time. But it is one hour earlier or later in the zones on either side.

How time zones work

Some very big countries, such as the United States of America, go across many time zones. America is made up of smaller parts called states. The time lines on this map bend to keep some whole states in one zone.

This way is West. Each zone is an hour earlier going this way.

This way is East. Each zone is an hour later going this way.

1 o'clock

2 o'clock

3 o'clock

4 o'clock

These lines show the time zones.

Saving daylight

In many places the Sun rises early in summer when most people are asleep. This seems a waste of daylight. So lots of places put their clocks forward one hour in summer.

Now the clocks say it is time to get up one hour earlier than in winter.

The clocks go back again one hour in winter.

Changing the time

When you travel into a new zone you change the time on your watch. You put it forward one hour for each zone you cross going East, and back one hour for each zone going West.

There is one special line called the International Date Line. When you cross it, you change the day of the week, as well as the time.

Internet link *Go to* ***www.usborne-quicklinks.com*** *for a link to a website where you can see what time it is now in other parts of the world.*

The seasons

As well as spinning around once each day, the Earth also moves around the Sun. It takes a year to go around once.

The Earth is not quite upright as it spins in space. It leans to one side.

North

North Pole

The top half is the Northern Hemisphere.

This imaginary line around the middle is the Equator.

The bottom half is the Southern Hemisphere.

South

South Pole

The way the Earth leans makes the seasons change in both hemispheres during the year.

The Sun's rays

The Sun's rays shine more directly on the half leaning towards it. Direct rays feel hot. It is summer here.

Direct ray

The Sun always shines almost directly on the Equator. It is always hot here.

Direct ray

The Sun's rays slant across the half leaning away from it. Slanting rays feel cooler than direct rays because their heat spreads over more ground. It is winter here.

Slanting ray

A journey around the Sun

Internet link Go to **www.usborne-quicklinks.com** *for a link to a website with an Earth and Moon activity.*

This picture shows the Earth moving around the Sun. The Earth always leans the same way so the Sun shines more directly on the Northern half and then on the Southern half. This gives each half summer and winter. When it is summer in one half, it is winter in the other.

Summer nights

The hemisphere that leans towards the Sun spends more time in sunlight each day. Nights are short.

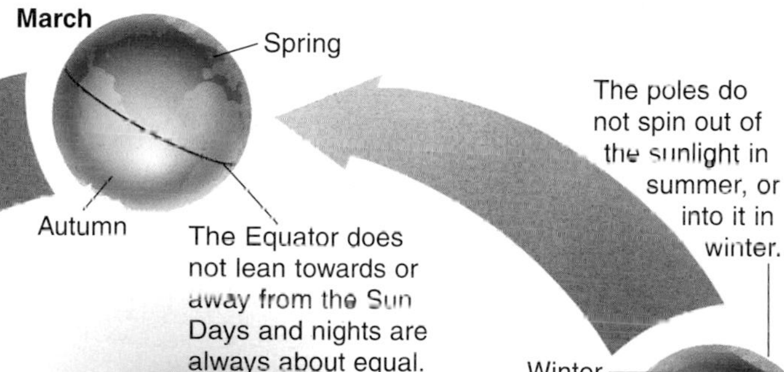

March
Spring
Autumn
The Equator does not lean towards or away from the Sun. Days and nights are always about equal.
The poles do not spin out of the sunlight in summer, or into it in winter.
Winter
December
Summer
June
Summer
Winter

Spring and autumn

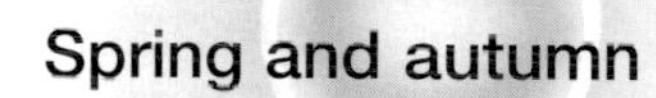

In the middle of spring and autumn neither half leans more towards the Sun. Days and nights are the same length.

Winter nights

The hemisphere that leans away from the Sun does not get many hours of light. Nights are long.

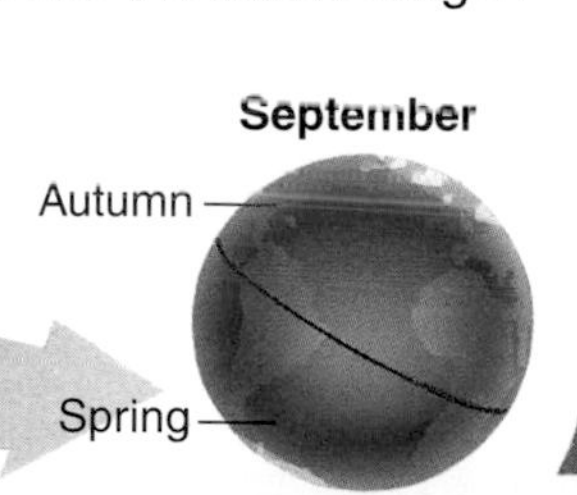

September
Autumn
Spring

The Moon

Some nights are less dark than others. On a clear night you can usually see the Moon shining brightly.

The Moon looks big and bright in the night sky. But unlike the Sun it does not make its own light.

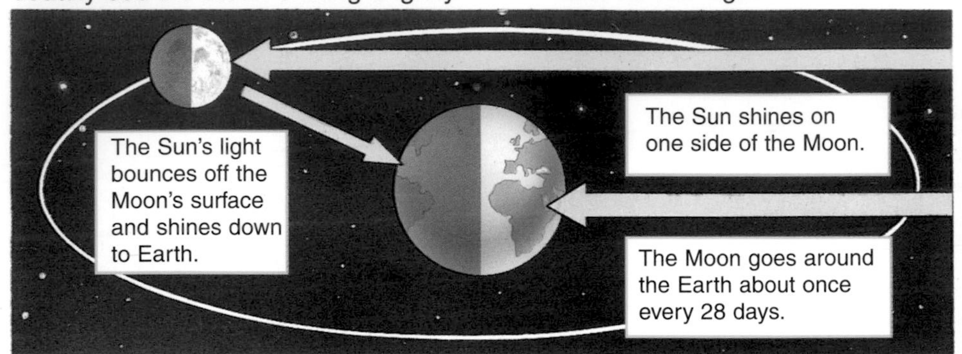

The Sun's light bounces off the Moon's surface and shines down to Earth.
The Sun shines on one side of the Moon.
The Moon goes around the Earth about once every 28 days.

The changing Moon

As the Moon moves you see different amounts of its light side. You could record the shapes on paper.

Draw the shape you see inside a circle. Do it each evening you see the Moon for 28 days. See how it changes.

You cannot really see a New Moon. The Sun lights up the other side.

This is a Crescent Moon. You can see a little of the Moon's light side.

This is a Full Moon. You see all of its light side. After this you see less.

Internet link *Go to* ***www.usborne-quicklinks.com*** *for a link to a website that will tell you what shape the Moon will be tonight.*

Exploring the Moon

The Moon is nearer to Earth than the Sun or stars. It is the first place that people have visited in space.

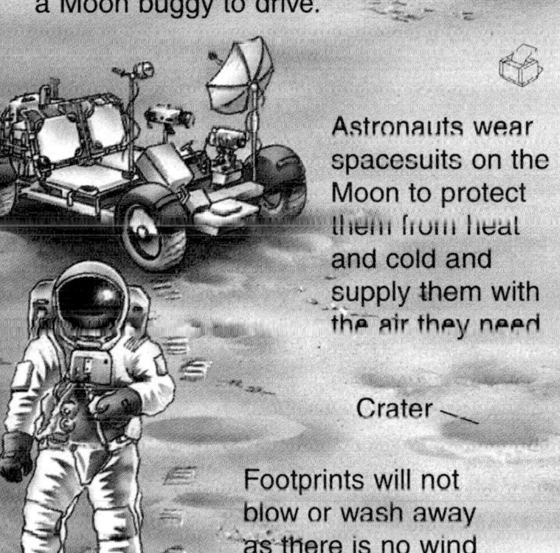

12 astronauts have been on the Moon so far, between 1969 and 1972. Some took a Moon buggy to drive.

Astronauts wear spacesuits on the Moon to protect them from heat and cold and supply them with the air they need.

Footprints will not blow or wash away as there is no wind or rain on the Moon.

There is no air, water or life on the Moon. It is a still and silent place, covered with craters made when space rocks crashed there.

The Man in the Moon

The dark patches you can see on the Moon are flat plains. Some people think they look like a face and call it the Man in the Moon. See if you can see it next time there is a Full Moon.

The Moon's pull

The Earth and Moon both pull things and people down towards them. This pull is called gravity. It makes things feel heavy when you lift them.

The Moon's pull is weaker than the Earth's. This makes things and people feel lighter there. Astronauts' spacesuits and backpacks are not so heavy on the Moon. Astronauts walk with great bouncy steps.

Internet link *Go to* ***www.usborne-quicklinks.com*** *for a link to a website where you can find out about the different parts of an astronaut's spacesuit.*

About the stars

On clear nights you can see hundreds of stars. Each one is a giant ball of hot, glowing gases like the Sun.

The stars look tiny because they are very far away.

The Sun is really a star too. It looks so big because it is our nearest star. Others are bigger but further away.

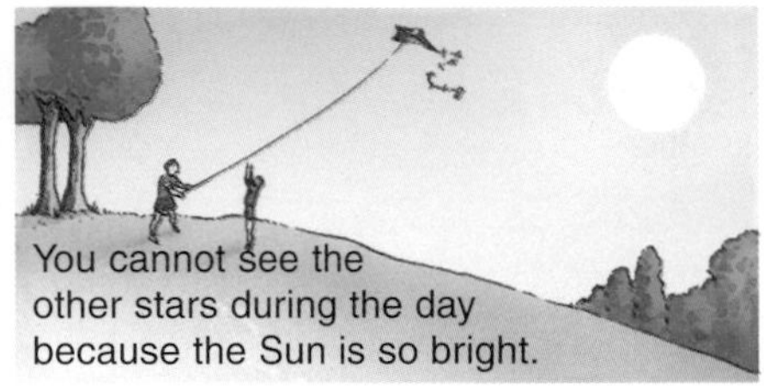

You cannot see the other stars during the day because the Sun is so bright.

A star is born

Stars are born in a gas and dust cloud. The cloud squeezes into a ball. It gets very hot and glows as a new star.

After millions of years a star swells up and cools. It is now called a red giant. Later, its outer layers drift into space.

Some of the biggest stars explode at the end of their lives. They leave behind new clouds of gas and dust.

A gas and dust cloud is called a nebula.

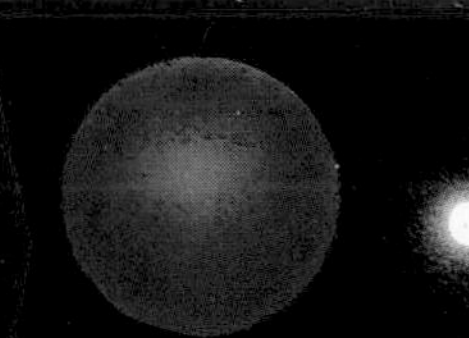

Red giants leave behind white dwarfs.

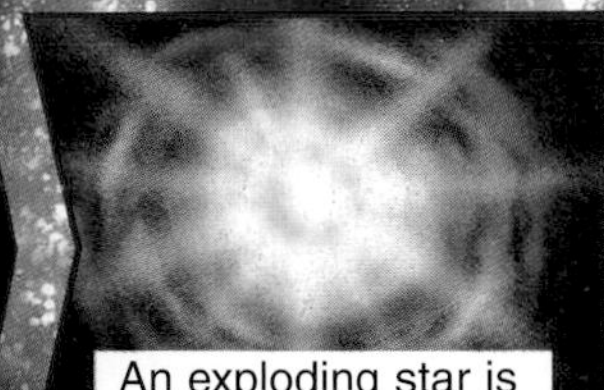

An exploding star is called a supernova.

Internet link *Go to* ***www.usborne-quicklinks.com*** *for a link to a website where you can find out about stars with an interactive photo quiz.*

The Milky Way

Stars belong to huge groups called galaxies. The stars you see belong to a galaxy called the Milky Way.

The Earth is also in the Milky Way.

The Milky Way is a spiral shape. It spins slowly through space.

The Sun is one of thousands of millions of stars in the Milky Way.

The Milky Way is one of thousands of millions of galaxies in space.

Star patterns

Long ago people saw patterns in the stars. These patterns are called constellations. You can see different ones from different parts of Earth.

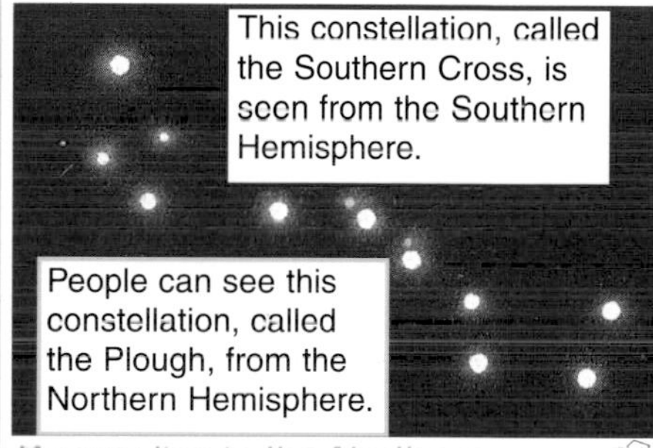

This constellation, called the Southern Cross, is seen from the Southern Hemisphere.

People can see this constellation, called the Plough, from the Northern Hemisphere.

Do you live in the Northern or Southern Hemisphere?

Sailing by the stars

The stars have always helped sailors find their way. The North Star shows which way is North, and two stars at the end of the Plough point to it.

The Solar System

Our part of the Milky Way is called the Solar System. The Sun is at the centre with nine planets and lots of moons and bits of rock going around it. You can see them in this picture.

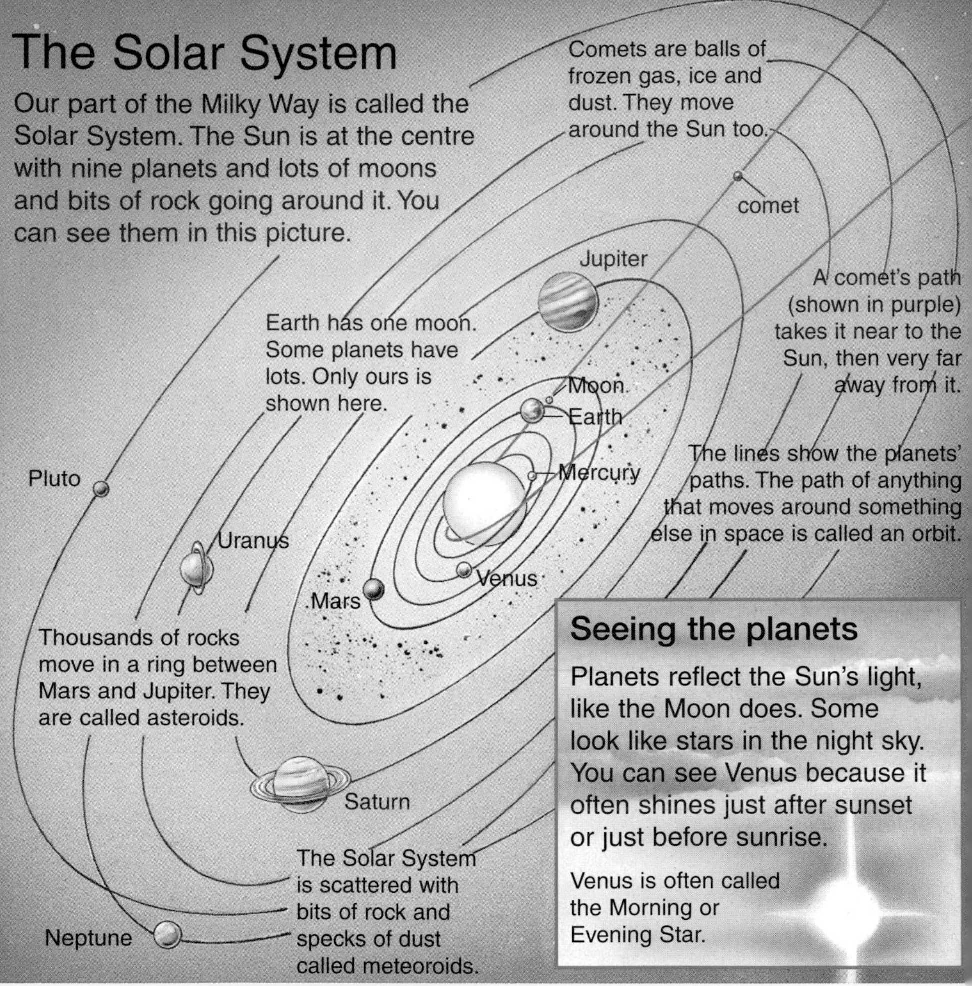

Comets are balls of frozen gas, ice and dust. They move around the Sun too.
comet
Jupiter
A comet's path (shown in purple) takes it near to the Sun, then very far away from it.
Earth has one moon. Some planets have lots. Only ours is shown here.
Moon
Earth
Mercury
The lines show the planets' paths. The path of anything that moves around something else in space is called an orbit.
Pluto
Uranus
Venus
Mars
Thousands of rocks move in a ring between Mars and Jupiter. They are called asteroids.
Saturn
The Solar System is scattered with bits of rock and specks of dust called meteoroids.
Neptune

Seeing the planets

Planets reflect the Sun's light, like the Moon does. Some look like stars in the night sky. You can see Venus because it often shines just after sunset or just before sunrise.

Venus is often called the Morning or Evening Star.

Internet link *Go to* ***www.usborne-quicklinks.com*** *for a link to a website with clickable facts about our Solar System.*

Night sights

Here are some other bright things you may see in the night sky. Some are natural and others are man-made.

As a comet gets near the Sun the gas and dust flow into a long, bright tail. You may very occasionally see one at night.

Sometimes meteoroids fall into the Earth's air. They burn up, making a bright streak called a meteor or shooting star.

A satellite is a spacecraft. It may send telephone calls, television pictures and other information around the world.

Satellites reflect sunlight and glint like slow-moving stars.

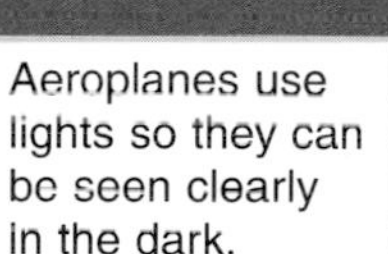

Aeroplanes use lights so they can be seen clearly in the dark.

Glowing lights

This coloured light is called an aurora.

It begins at about 96 kilometres (60 miles) above the ground.

Sometimes the Sun gives out extra bursts of energy. These can make the sky near the poles glow with slowly changing colours.

Town lights reflect off clouds. They can make the sky glow.

People light fireworks at night as they show up best in the dark.

Internet link *Go to* ***www.usborne-quicklinks.com*** *for a link to a website where you can find lots of photographs and facts about auroras.*

Night life

Some animals come out at night. Most can see well in the dark, and have a good sense of hearing, smell or touch, too. These senses warn them of danger and help them to find food and mates in the dark.

Here you can see some animals that come out when it starts to get dark. These animals are nocturnal, which means "of the night".

Most bats cannot see well. Some have a special kind of hearing to help them catch moths at night.

Badgers sniff the air for danger before leaving their burrows. The damp night air carries smells well.

Rabbits and deer go further afield at night. The dark helps to hide them from enemies.

Cats and foxes use their long whiskers to feel their way through small gaps.

Owls and cats have big eyes that open up in the dark to let in as much light as possible.

Hedgehogs use their snouts to smell and forage for grubs.

Internet link *Go to* ***www.usborne-quicklinks.com*** *for a link to a website where you can find fascinating facts and pictures of nocturnal animals.*

Noises at night

The dark hides friends as well as enemies. Some animals find mates by calling to them.

Frogs croak to let other frogs know where they are.

A male cricket makes a chirping call to a female by rubbing its wings together.

Bat squeaks

Bat squeaks make echoes as they bounce off things such as trees. Bats listen to the echoes to find out where things are.

Bats do not bump into things. They zigzag to avoid trees, or to catch insects.

Most bat noises are too high for people to hear.

Glowing in the night

Some insects have a special way of making light in their own bodies.

Glow-worms shine in the dark to attract mates.

Fire-flies flash light to each other.

Honey mushrooms also glow at night on rotting wood.

Flowers of the night

Some flowers are also nocturnal. They smell sweeter at night.

The scent attracts moths that get food from the flowers.

Moths also take pollen from one flower to another. This helps new flowers grow.

Night-flowering catchfly

Internet link *Go to* ***www.usborne-quicklinks.com*** *for a link to a website where you can listen to bats and search for insects in the night.*

How light works

During the day, the Sun's light lets you see shapes and colours.

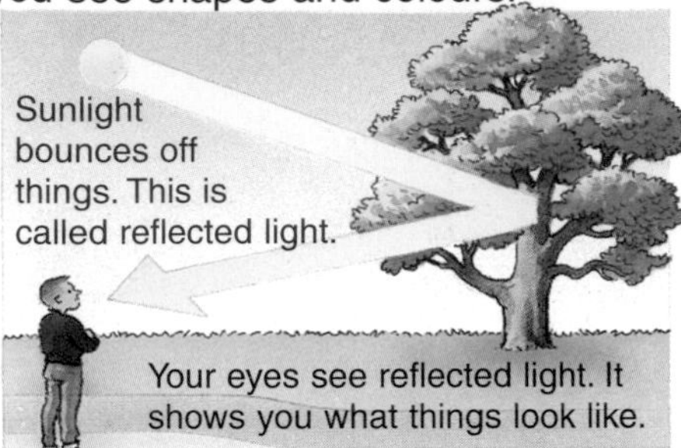

Sunlight bounces off things. This is called reflected light.
Your eyes see reflected light. It shows you what things look like.

At night there is not enough light to see things clearly.

People travelling at night use lights to see and be seen.

Light and colour

Sunlight looks clear but is really made up of many colours. You can see them when the Sun shines through raindrops and makes a rainbow.

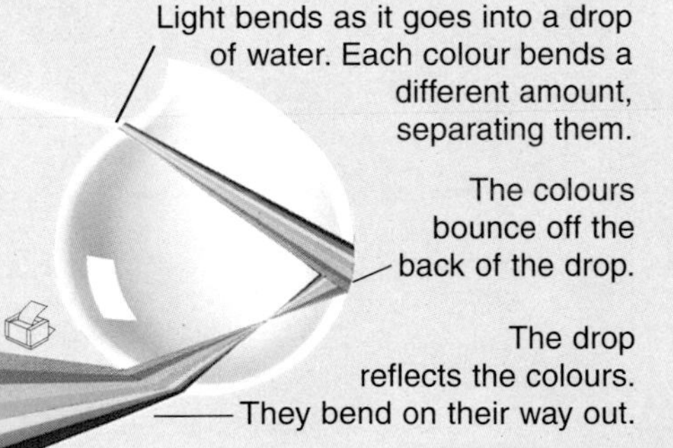

Light bends as it goes into a drop of water. Each colour bends a different amount, separating them.
The colours bounce off the back of the drop.
The drop reflects the colours. They bend on their way out.

A green leaf only reflects the green colour in sunlight. It takes in, or absorbs, the rest.

That is why a leaf looks green.

Light gives all things their colour. When light hits things, some colours are reflected. The rest are taken in. You only see the reflected colours.

Make a colour mixer

You can see how lots of colours mix to make white. Cut out a card circle 10cm (4in) across. Lightly crayon in the rainbow colours.

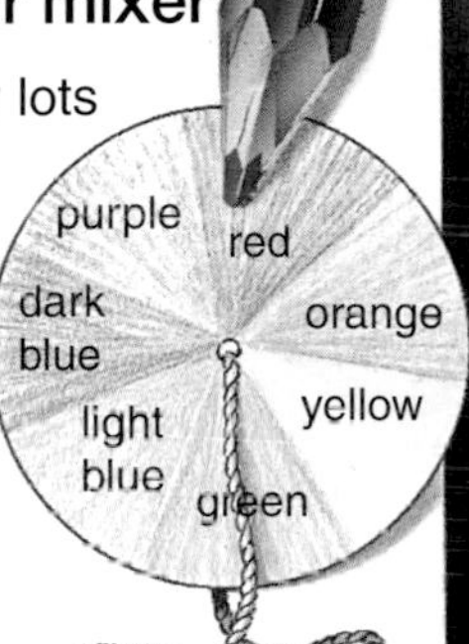

Thread some string through the centre.

Hold each end loosely. Swing the card around in big loops.

Pull both ends tight so the card spins fast. Look at the colours as the card spins.

The colours blend. If you spin the card very fast it looks almost white.

Why is sky blue?

In the day the sky is often blue, because there is a layer of air around the Earth.

This air is full of dust and drops of water. These scatter the blue colour in sunlight more than the other colours.

There is no air in space to scatter the Sun's light. This is why space is black.

A black sky

The sky above the Moon is black even during the day because there is no layer of air around it.

Internet link *Go to* ***www.usborne-quicklinks.com*** *for a link to a website where you can follow an online investigation about light.*

Shadows

Light only moves in straight lines. It leaves dark shadows behind things that stand in its way. That is why the Earth is always dark on one side. The Sun's light cannot bend around it.

Draw your shadow

On a sunny day, you stop some sunlight reaching the ground. This makes your shadow.

Ask a friend to draw around your shadow on a sunny morning.

Mark where you stood. Do it again at other times of the day.

Midday

Evening

Shadows always point away from the Sun.

See how your shadow moves and how long it gets, as the Sun moves across the sky.

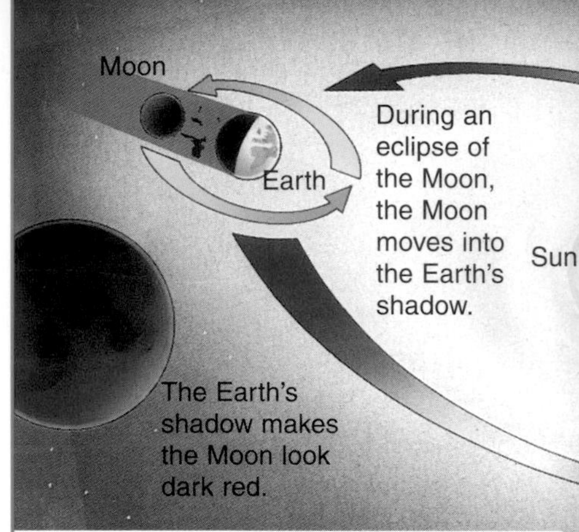
Moon
Earth
Sun
During an eclipse of the Moon, the Moon moves into the Earth's shadow.
The Earth's shadow makes the Moon look dark red.

The Earth's shadow

At times the Earth is directly between the Sun and the Moon. The Sun's rays cannot bend around to light the Moon. This is an eclipse of the Moon.

Day shadows

The Sun's rays reach the ground in a short, more direct path.

This makes short shadows.

Shadows are short at midday when the Sun is high in the sky.

 Internet links *Go to* ***www.usborne-quicklinks.com*** *for links to websites where you can watch an animation of an eclipse and explore online shadow activities.*

The sky grows dark for a few minutes and the stars appear.

he Moon's Shadow

ess often, the Moon moves directly etween the Earth and Sun. It blocks it the Sun and casts a shadow on e Earth. This is an eclipse of the Sun.

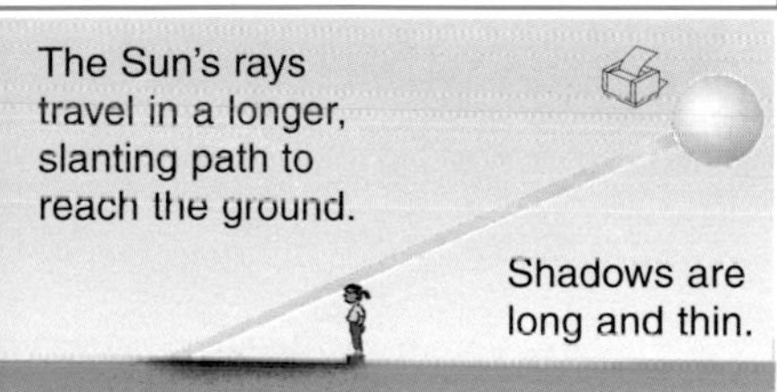

The Sun's rays travel in a longer, slanting path to reach the ground.
Shadows are long and thin.

Shadows are long in the morning and evening, when the Sun is low.

Make a shadow clock

Fix a pencil upright on a piece of card, with Plasticine. Leave it in a sunny place in the morning.

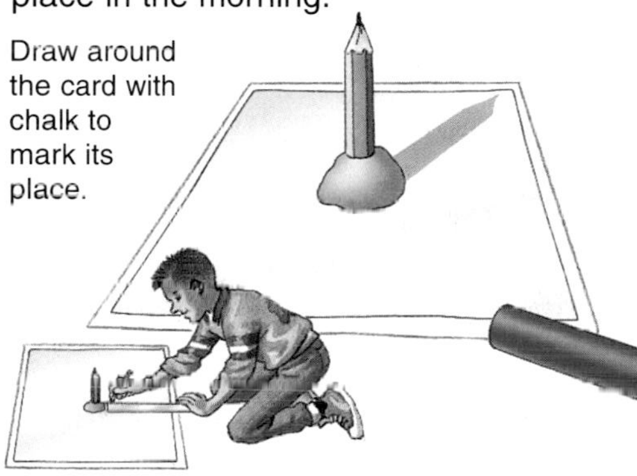

Draw around the card with chalk to mark its place.

Draw the pencil's shadow. Write the time by the shadow. Do this again every hour.

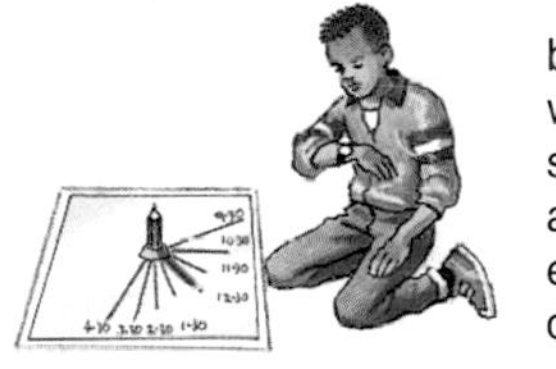

This clock will only be right for a few weeks. The shadows change as the Sun rises earlier or later during the year.

Put the card in the same position the next day. The shadow will show you roughly what time it is.

Electric lights

People have only used electric light bulbs for about 120 years. The first one was made by Thomas Edison in 1879. Here you see what happens when you turn on a light or torch.

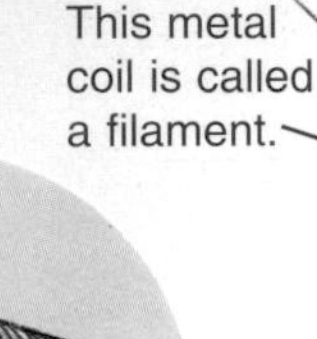

This metal coil is called a filament.

A torch makes a strong, steady beam.

A battery inside the torch sends electricity to light up the bulb. When all the electricity is used up, you can put in a new battery.

Electric bulbs are much stronger and brighter than any light used before.

Electricity goes along hidden wires to the light bulb. It makes a metal coil inside the bulb glow white hot.

Guiding lights

At night, lighthouses warn ships of rocks with a strong, flashing light.

"Cat's-eyes" are bits of glass set in rubber blocks.

"Cat's-eyes" in roads reflect car lights back to the driver.

Bright lights on the runway help aeroplanes land when it is dark.

Internet link *Go to* ***www.usborne-quicklinks.com*** *for a link to a website where you can find out more about the invention of the light bulb.*